Jewel Box Quilt

by Eleanor Burns

For Marie Elise Sammet Knoechel

First printing February, 1997
Published by Quilt in a Day®, Inc.
1955 Diamond St. San Marcos, CA 92069

©1997-Eleanor A. Burns Family Trust

ISBN 0-922705-91-7

Editor Eleanor Burns
Assistant Editor Robin Green
Art Director Merritt Voigtlander
Assistant Art Director Susan Sells

Table of Contents

Introduction

Marie Elise Sammet Knoechel, my paternal grandmother, set her foot on American soil in December, 1929. As she passed through the turnstile on Ellis Island, she was grateful to be on land after a stormy journey. Her small daughter, Annelise, and young son Erwin, were safe with her. Elise searched the crowds for her husband Martin, who had built a new life for them in Zelienople, Pennsylvania. Safely pinned within the folds of her petticoat were their family jewels, carefully carried from their home town of Rehau, Germany.

Those family jewels were far more than pieces of precious stones and metals. They were the stones of her life passed on to her two children and eight grandchildren. My sisters say I am much like my grandmother. I'm certainly happy when my chicken soup tastes just like hers!

One of the most precious metals Grandma passed on to me was gold – beautiful gold painted on fine porcelain dinnerware. The gold trim was lovingly painted by her sister-in law, Tana Anna Woefel. Tiny delicate flowers in colors of ruby, sapphire, emerald, and amethyst grace this fine porcelain. Alise passed on a treasure of lovely jewels of beauty and tradition.

It's the same warmth for tradition I feel when I create a quilt. The Jewel Box is the perfect quilt to make from the "scraps of your life." Stitch in a treasured piece of fabric from your grandmother, or your sister or your child! You can sew the family jewels right into your quilt! You will love the easy way the pieces fit together!

Create a new tradition for your family. Pass on a treasure!

Eleanor Burns

About the Quilt

Four basic units make up the Jewel Box quilt:
- ❖ the Pieced Square,
- ❖ the Four-Patch,
- ❖ the Framing Border,
- ❖ and the Piano Keys Border.

Each block is made of eight different Four-Patches, and eight different Pieced Squares. Finished size of a block is 16". The quilt takes on its jewel like quality from the multitude of mediums and darks set against one background.

Depending on the fabric you use, there are two different methods given for cutting and sewing the basic units. Yardage Charts list both for each size quilt.
- ❖ Strips
- ❖ Charm Squares and Scraps

Strips

Use the Strip method if you choose to purchase all new yardage, or already have a stash of fabric with pieces no less than 5½" wide selvage to selvage. It's the fastest, easiest method! Even though the Jewel Box quilt calls for up to twenty-five different fabrics, each fabric is used equally, so there is very little waste.

Piano Keys   4   4

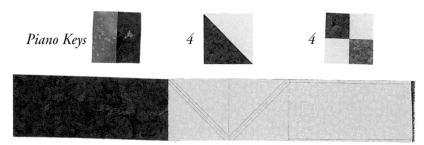

Yardage is cut into 5½" strips selvage to selvage. Half of a 5½" background strip is sewn with a 5½" medium or dark strip to yield four Pieced Squares and four Four-Patches. The remaining half of the medium or dark strip is used for the Piano Keys border. You may substitute half strips for more variety. From one fat quarter, you can get three 5½" half strips. The length of the half strip should be at least 21½".

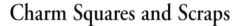

Charm Squares and Scraps

Quilters often collect and trade 5½" and 6" squares with friends and quilt guild members. These squares are referred to as Charm Squares. Mail order fabric clubs also send out swatches of their fabrics so you can see the quality and colors before making your purchase. These squares may not be perfect in measurement. Fortunately, with this method, accuracy in the original size is not that critical.

Jewel Box is the perfect quilt for utilizing the wide range of colors you may have collected. Use one background fabric to help tie them together. In addition, you can cut 5½" squares from your scraps to add to your Charms.

In this method, each 5½" background square sewn with a 5½" medium or dark square yields two Pieced Squares or two Four-Patches. The Piano Keys border is made from 2½" wide strips.

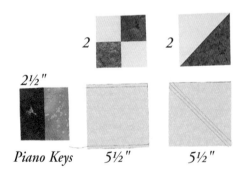

Piano Keys   *5½"*   *5½"*

Instructions for full size quilts are written using 5½" squares. However, if your charms are 6", it's not necessary to trim them until after sewing. Cut the background to 6" as well. Charm Squares 4" and smaller can be used to make the Miniature Quilt featured on page 58.

This method takes time to organize and cut the fabric squares. However, you can use up small scraps in a multitude of colors. You will no doubt have various grades of fabric in your collection, and they all work differently. The techniques used will help to compensate for this variety.

Color and Fabric Selection

Select one background fabric in 100% cotton, such as plain quilter's muslin, a tone on tone, or a sparsely scattered light background print. The background fabric should be at least 43½" in width.

Medium and dark cottons can be large or small scale prints, tone on tone, or checks. Contrast is most important.

If you have purchased kits with strips or charm squares, do not pre-wash. After the quilt is completed, wash with ¼ cup white vinegar to set colors.

With changes in fabric lines, the quilt takes on a different look. The possibilities are endless. The fabric selection often suggests one of the alternate names for Jewel Box.

Going to Chicago and *World's Fair* were two of the names given to this block in the 1930's. Reproduction fabrics give the quilt a light and airy quality.

Because it is sewn from four quarter blocks, the Jewel Box is especially easy to "customize." The placement of mediums and darks in center squares can be adjusted by the arrangement of your blocks. Lay out the whole quilt and balance colors in all the blocks, or sew quarters randomly for a scrappier feel.

By balancing the placement of mediums and darks in the center squares, the Jewel Box becomes an *Hour Glass*.

The Jewel Box has also been called the *Gay Scrap Quilt*. Using different lights for your background is one way to give your quilt an extra scrappy feel.

Four-patches make chains around the matched center squares of this Planned Jewel Box for a *Railroad Crossing*.

Yardage

Finishes approximately 44" x 44"

Wallhanging *Four Blocks*

 Pieced Squares

 Four-Patches

Framing Border

 Piano Keys Border

Purchase yardage or use Charm Squares and Scraps.

Purchased Yardage

Cut strips selvage to selvage

Dark and Medium Prints *Assorted*	(10) ¼ yd pieces	(1) 5½" wide strip from each print or (10) 5½" wide strips total or (20) 5½" wide half strips total
Background *at least 43½" wide* Framing Border	1 yd	(4) 5½" wide strips (4) 2½" wide strips

---

or Charm Squares and Scraps

Dark and Medium Prints *Assorted*		(32) 5½" squares (12) 2½" wide strips or (24) 2½" wide half strips
Background *at least 43½" wide* Framing Border	1⅓ yd	(6) 5½" wide strips (4) 2½" wide strips

---

Borders and Finishing

Binding	⅝ yd	(5) 3" wide strips
Backing	3 yds or 48" sq.	cut into (2) equal pieces
Bonded Batting	52" x 52"	

Crib *Six Blocks*

 Pieced Squares

 Four-Patches

 Framing Border

 Piano Keys Border

Finishes approximately 44" x 64"

Purchase yardage or use Charm Squares and Scraps.

Purchased Yardage

Cut strips selvage to selvage

Dark and Medium Prints *Assorted*	(16) ¼ yd pieces	(1) 5½" wide strip from each print or (16) 5½" wide strips total or (32) 5½" wide half strips total
Background *at least 43½" wide* Framing Border	1½ yds	(6) 5½" wide strips (5) 2½" wide strips

or Charm Squares and Scraps

Dark and Medium Prints *Assorted*	(48) 5½" squares (20) 2½" wide strips or (40) 2½" wide half strips
Background *at least 43½" wide* Framing Border	1¾ yds (8) 5½" wide strips (5) 2½" wide strips

Borders and Finishing

Binding	⅝ yd	(6) 3" wide strips
Backing	3 yds	cut into (2) equal pieces
Bonded Batting	52" x 68"	

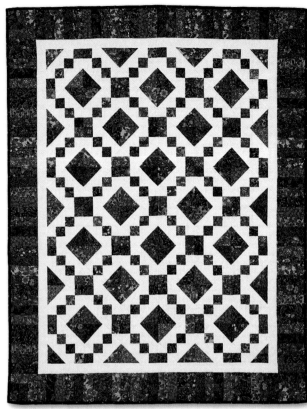

Finishes approximately 64" x 80"

Lap Robe *Twelve Blocks*

 Pieced Squares

 Four-Patches

Framing Border

 Piano Keys Border

Purchase yardage or use Charm Squares and Scraps.

Purchased Yardage

Cut strips selvage to selvage

Dark and Medium Prints
Assorted (24) ¼ yd pieces (1) 5½" wide strip from each print
or (24) 5½" wide strips total
or (48) 5½" wide half strips total

Background *at least 43½" wide* 2½ yds (12) 5½" wide strips
Framing Border (6) 2½" wide strips

or Charm Squares and Scraps

Dark and Medium Prints
Assorted (96) 5½" squares
(24) 2½" wide strips
or (48) 2½" wide half strips

Background *at least 43½" wide* 2¾ yds (14) 5½" wide strips
Framing Border (6) 2½" wide strips

Finishing

Binding ⅔ yd (7) 3" wide strips
Backing 4 yds cut into (2) equal pieces
Bonded Batting 68" x 84"

Finishes approximately 64" x 96"

Twin *Fifteen Blocks*

 Pieced Squares

 Four-Patches

 Framing Border

 Piano Keys Border

Purchase yardage or use Charm Squares and Scraps.

Purchased Yardage

Cut strips selvage to selvage

Dark and Medium Prints *Assorted*	(15) ⅜ yd pieces	(2) 5½" wide strips from each print or (30) 5½" wide strips total or (60) 5½" wide half strips total
Background *at least 43½" wide* Framing Border	3 yds	(15) 5½" wide strips (7) 2½" wide strips

or Charm Squares and Scraps

Dark and Medium Prints *Assorted*		(120) 5½" squares (28) 2½" wide strips or (56) 2½" wide half strips
Background *at least 43½" wide* Framing Border	3½ yds	(18) 5½" wide strips (7) 2½" wide strips

Finishing

Binding	¾ yd	(8) 3" wide strips
Backing	6 yds	cut into (2) equal pieces
Bonded Batting	68" x 100"	

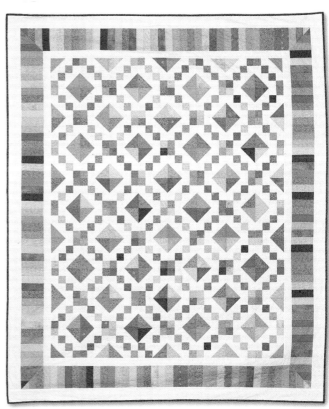

Double finishes approximately 80" x 96"
Queen finishes approximately 86" x 103"

Double/Queen *Twenty Blocks*

 Pieced Squares

 Four-Patches

Framing Border

 Piano Keys Border

Purchase yardage or use Charm Squares and Scraps.

Purchased Yardage

Cut strips selvage to selvage

| Dark and Medium Prints *Assorted* | (20) ⅜ yd pieces | (2) 5½" wide strips from each print or (40) 5½" wide strips total or (80) 5½" wide half strips total |
| Background   *at least 43½" wide* Framing Border | 4 yds | (20) 5½" wide strips (8) 2½" wide strips |

---

or Charm Squares and Scraps

| Dark and Medium Prints *Assorted* | | (160) 5½" squares (32) 2½" wide strips or (64) 2½" wide half strips |
| Background   *at least 43½" wide* Framing Border | 4½ yds | (24) 5½" wide strips (8) 2½" wide strips |

Finishing

Outside Border - Queen only	1⅛ yds	(9) 4" wide strips
Binding	1 yd	(10) 3" wide strips
Backing	6 yds	cut into (2) equal pieces
Bonded Batting	100" x 104"	

13

King *Twenty-five Blocks*

 Pieced Squares

 Four-Patches

 Framing Border

 Piano Keys Border

Finishes approximately 102" x 102"

Purchase yardage or use Charm Squares and Scraps.

Purchased Yardage

	Cut strips selvage to selvage	
Dark and Medium Prints *Assorted*	(25) ⅜ yd pieces	(2) 5½" wide strips from each print or (50) 5½" wide strips total or (100) 5½" wide half strips total
Background *at least 43½" wide* Framing Border	5 yds	(25) 5½" wide strips (9) 2½" wide strips

---

or Charm Squares and Scraps

Dark and Medium Prints *Assorted*		(200) 5½" squares (32) 2½" wide strips or (64) 2½" wide half strips
Background *at least 43½" wide* Framing Border	5½ yds	(30) 5½" wide strips (9) 2½" wide strips

---

Finishing

Outside Border *optional*	1⅓ yds	(11) 4" wide strips
Binding	1 yd	(11) 3" wide strips
Backing	9 yds	cut into (3) equal pieces
Bonded Batting	108" x 108"	

• Supplies

Rotary Cutter

Ruler/Cutter

Rulers

6" x 6"

6" x 12"

12½" Square Up

6" x 24"

Compare measurements on rulers and cutting mat to each other. Make certain that the measurements match.

Seam Guide

Pressing Mat and Iron

Cutting Mat

Darning Foot

1" Safety Pins

Walking Foot

Kwik Klip™

Hera Marker

Grey Thread

Invisible Thread

Marking Pencil

Stiletto

Cutting & Sewing

Cutting Strips

Use a large rotary cutter with a sharp blade and a 6" x 24" plexiglass ruler on a gridded cutting mat. Check that the measurements are the same on the rulers and the gridded cutting mat.

Cut strips selvage to selvage. **Do not cut off selvage edges.** Fabrics now come in widths from 40" to 45" wide. On very narrow yardage, every ¼" is needed! Pay particular attention to instructions regarding selvage placement.

A ruler/cutter combination tool can also be used in the same manner as the two separate tools.

1. Fold the fabric in half, and place on the mat with the fold at the top.

2. Line up the edge of the fabric on the gridded cutting mat with the left edge extended slightly to the left of zero. Reverse this procedure if you are left-handed.

3. Line up the 6" x 24" ruler on zero. Spread the fingers of your left hand to hold the ruler firmly. With the rotary cutter in your right hand, begin cutting with the blade against the ruler. Put all your strength into the rotary cutter as you cut away from you, and straighten the edge.

4. Lift, and move the ruler until it lines up with the width of the strip on the grid and cut. Open and check to see that it is straight. Lift, and move to the next given width. Cut again.

Strips for Blocks:	Cut 5½" wide strips. Refer to your Yardage Chart for the number of 5½" strips to cut.
Borders:	Framing Borders are cut 2½" wide. Queen and King Outside Borders are cut 4" wide.

5. Open and check strips periodically. Make a straightening cut when necessary.

Cutting Background Strips into Squares

Method One

Leave the strips in place on the cutting mat. With the 6" x 24" ruler, trim the selvage edges. Cut strips into squares.

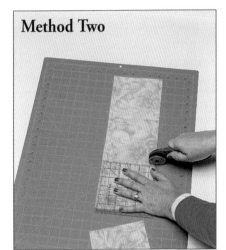

Method Two

Stack several strips. With the 6" square ruler, square off the left selvage edges. Move ruler to designated measurement, and layer cut squares.

Cutting Squares from Dark and Medium Scraps

1. Layer fabric pieces larger than 5½", matching grain lines. Pull a thread to see grain. Press.

2. Place the fabric on a small cutting mat or turn table so squares can be rotated while cutting.

3. Center the 6" square ruler on the stack. Line up the edges of the ruler with the grain lines. Cut two sides.

4. Turn and cut the remaining two sides to 5½" square.

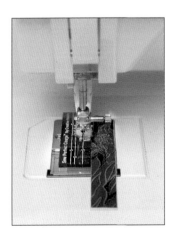

Seam Allowance

Use an accurate ¼" seam. A fabric guide placed ¼" from needle is helpful when sewing Four-Patches, blocks and Piano Keys.

Making Pieces from Strips

Marking the Background Strips

1. Measure your background strip. It should be at least 43½" wide. **Do not cut off selvages.**

2. Count out this many 5½" wide background strips for your size quilt:

Quilt Size	Strips
Wallhanging	4
Crib	6
Lap Robe	12
Twin	15
Dble-Queen	20
King	25

3. Carefully line up the selvage edges, and press each strip in half.

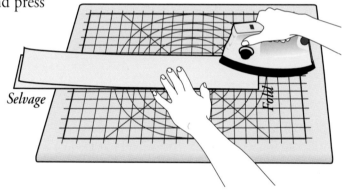

4. Place the gridded cutting mat on the table with zero in the bottom left corner.

5. Place the folded strip on the gridded cutting mat.

6. **Sliver trim the folded edge** with the 12½" Square Up ruler.

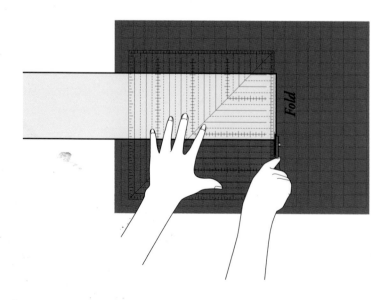

7. Place the cut edges of both strips on zero with wrong sides up.

8. Measure and mark at 5½" and 11" using the grid on the mat.

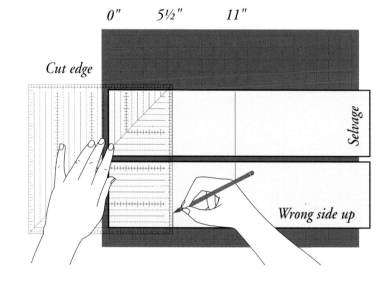

9. Draw continuous diagonal lines across the 5½" squares.

10. You need this many half strips for your size quilt:

Quilt Size	Half Strips
Wallhanging	8
Crib	12
Lap Robe	24
Twin	30
Dble-Queen	40
King	50

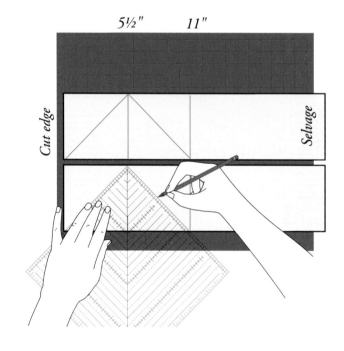

11. Measure the half strip. It should be at least 21½".

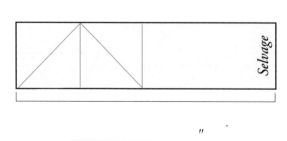

Layering Strips for the Blocks

1. Count out this many dark and medium 5½" wide strips for your size quilt:

Quilt Size	Strips
Wallhanging	8*
Crib	12*
Lap Robe	24*
Twin	30*
Dble-Queen	40*
King	50*

*Half Strips for Blocks

Half Strips for blocks should be at least 21½".
Save half strips shorter than 21½" for Piano Keys.
Refer to step number six for instructions.

2. Stack up several dark and medium selvage to selvage strips on pressing mat. Carefully line up selvages on right. Press out folds.

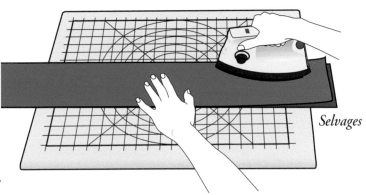

Selvages

Because of varying widths of fabric, left selvages do not need to line up.

3. Place stack on cutting mat with lined up selvages on right.

4. Cut dark and medium strips same length as background strip, approximately 21½".

5. Set aside the remaining half for the piano keys.

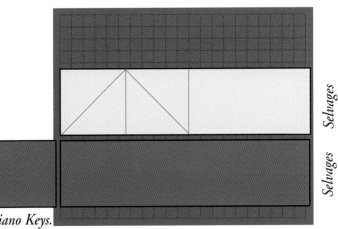

Selvages

Selvages

Reserve for Piano Keys.
They only need to be 20" in length.

Cut same length as background strip

6. Pin a background strip with each dark or medium strip, right sides together.

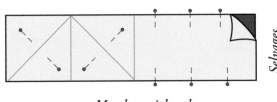

Selvages

Match straight edges.

Sewing the Layered Strips

1. Thread your sewing machine with thread a slightly darker shade than the background color. Grey is often a good color.

2. Sew an accurate ¼" seam allowance, and 15 stitches to the inch, or a #2 setting.

   Start sewing at 1, pull the threads to 2, and continue sewing and pivoting to the end.

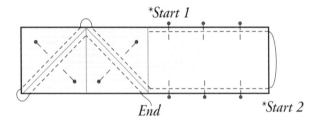

3. Cut the looping threads. Remove pins.

4. Press to set the seams.

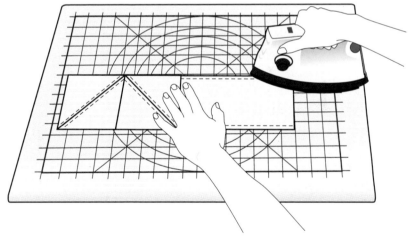

5. Cut into two sections.

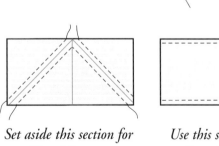

Set aside this section for Pieced Squares.   *Use this section for Four-Patches.*

Making Four-Patches

1. Examine the 6" x 12" ruler.
   Find the 2¼" lines.

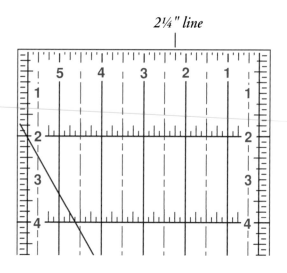

2¼" line

2. Place the **2¼" lines** of the 6" x 12" ruler
   on the stitching or thread line. Cut off strip.
   Stack.

   *If you sewed a perfect ¼" seam, the fabric's
   edge is at 2½".*

3. Repeat on the other half. Make second stack.

4. Both strips should measure 2¼" from the
   stitching or 2½" wide from edge to edge.

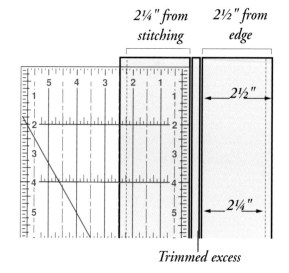

2¼" from stitching *2½" from edge*

2½"

2¼"

Trimmed excess

5. Lay on the pressing mat with darker strip on
   top. Line up strip with grid. Press open,
   seam allowance to the dark side. Carefully
   press out folds at the seams.

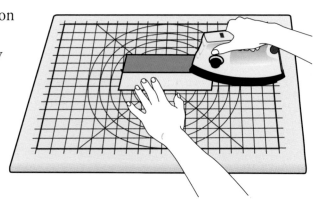

6. As you press, sort strips into two stacks. Make one stack with selvage edges on right and one stack with selvage edges on left.

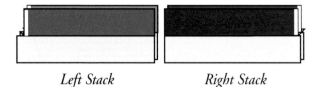

Left Stack   *Right Stack*

Pay particular attention to selvage placement.

If possible, place your cutting mat next to the sewing machine.

7. Work with **left stack** first. From left stack, take two sets of strips. Place on mat with **light strip on top**. Line up strips with the grid.

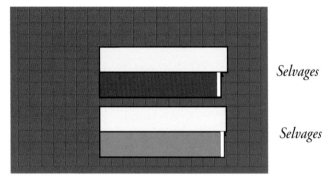

Selvages

Selvages

Follow illustrations exactly to end up with locking seams.

8. From the same stack, choose a second set of strips of **different fabrics**. Place right sides together with dark against background. Line up straight edges and selvages.

9. Lock the seams by pushing them together with your fingers. Trim left ends straight.

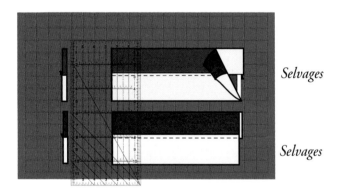

Selvages

Selvages

10. Find the **2½" line** on your ruler.

11. Cut **four 2½" layered pieces** from each of the paired strips. Lift and move the ruler as you cut.

Cut 2½" layered sections

12. Stack pairs with dark/medium at top. If necessary, lay the pieces on another ruler for easy transporting to the sewing machine.

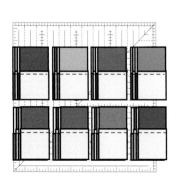

13. Repeat with right stack. Place two sets of strips on mat with **dark strips on top.**

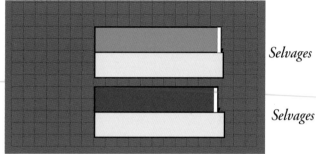

Selvages

Selvages

14. Place different strips right sides together with background against dark.

15. Trim left ends straight. Cut **four 2½" layered pairs** from each. Stack with dark at top.

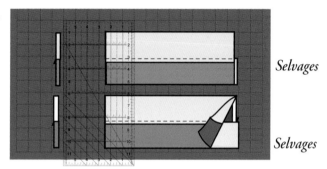

Selvages

Selvages

Cut 2½" layered sections

Sewing Pairs

1. Place a ¼" seam guide on machine. Sew a perfect ¼" seam allowance on one Four-Patch. Check the width of the new seam against the width of the first seam. They must match.

2. Assembly-line sew layered pieces. Use the stiletto to hold the seams flat as you sew over them.

Sew with dark/medium at top. The top seam butts into the seam underneath. Seams will also lock when sewing the block together.

3. Place Four-Patch on pressing mat with seam across the bottom. Press to set the seam. Open and press. Clip threads. Stack in groups of four.

4. Measure several Four-Patches. They should measure approximately 4½" square.

Your measurement: _____"

Because of this method, very seldom do the Four-Patches need to be squared. In that rare situation, sliver trim all sides evenly to a uniform size. The Pieced Squares will be squared to this same size.

5. You need this many Four-Patches for your size quilt:

Quilt Size	Four-Patches
Wallhanging	32
Crib	48
Lap Robe	96
Twin	120
Dble-Queen	160
King	200

If you were unable to get the required number, cut and sew additional 5½" squares. See page 27.

Making Pieced Squares

1. Cut on the diagonal lines with the 12½" Square Up ruler.

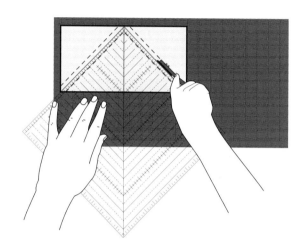

2. Cut on the straight line.

3. Stack.

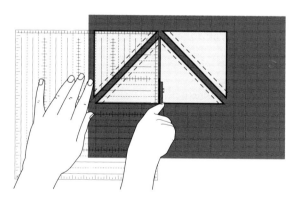

4. Lay the triangle on the pressing mat, dark side up. Press to set seam.

5. Open and press seam to dark side.

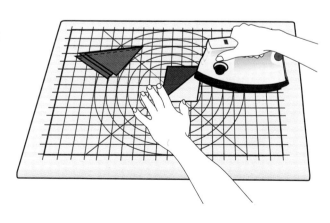

6. With a 6" x 6" ruler, square one Pieced Square to the size of your Four-Patch.

   Center the ruler's diagonal line on the seam, and trim two edges.

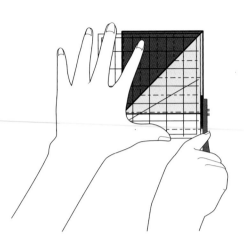

7. Turn the Pieced Square and lay the diagonal line on the seam.

   If your Four-Patch is 4⅜", place the 4⅜" ruler lines on the newly cut edges. Trim the final edges.

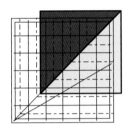

   If your Four-Patch is 4½", place the 4½" ruler lines on the newly cut edges. Trim the final edges.

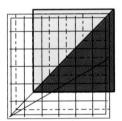

8. Compare with Four-Patch.

   Be satisfied with size of Pieced Square before trimming all of the pieces.

9. Square up this many Pieced Squares for your size quilt:

Quilt Size	Pieced Squares
Wallhanging	32
Crib	48
Lap Robe	96
Twin	120
Dble-Queen	160
King	200

Turn to page 32 to finish your blocks.

Pieces from Charm Squares & Scraps

Divide the medium and dark 5½" squares into two equal stacks. Make sure colors are divided evenly between the two stacks. Count out this many 5½" squares for each stack:

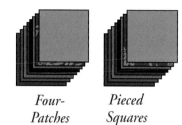

Four-Patches   Pieced Squares

Quilt Size	Squares per Stack
Wallhanging	16
Crib	24
Lap Robe	48
Twin	60
Dble-Queen	80
King	100

Making Four-Patches

1. Count out this many 5½" background strips for your size quilt:

Quilt Size	Strips
Wallhanging	3
Crib	4
Lap Robe	7
Twin	9
Dble-Queen	12
King	15

2. Thread your machine with a color slighter darker than the background color.

3. Place a dark/medium square right sides together to background strip. Sew down right side.

4. Place a second square next to the first, and continue to sew a ¼" seam.

5. Assembly-line sew all squares for Four-Patches.

6. Turn and sew a ¼" seam on second side.

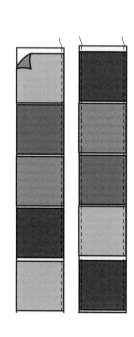

7. Press to set seams.

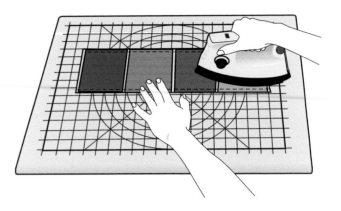

8. With a 6" x 12" ruler, cut background fabric apart between every two.

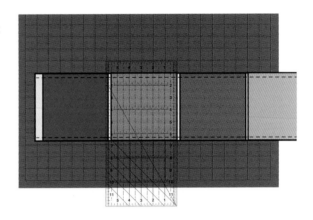

9. Examine the 6" x 12" ruler. Find the **2¼" lines**.

10. Place the 2¼" lines of the 6" x 12" ruler on the **stitching or thread line**. Cut off strip. If you sewed a perfect ¼" seam, the ruler's edge is at 2½".

11. Repeat on the other half.

12. Both strips should measure 2¼" from the stitching or 2½" wide from edge to edge.

13. Lay on the pressing mat with the darker strips on top. Press open, seam allowance to the dark side.

14. Cut apart between blocks.

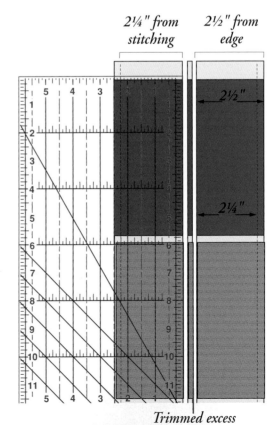

2¼" from stitching   *2½" from edge*

2½"

2¼"

Trimmed excess

Layering Strips

If possible, place your cutting mat next to the sewing machine.

1. Place two sets of strips on mat with **light strip on top**. Line up with the grid.

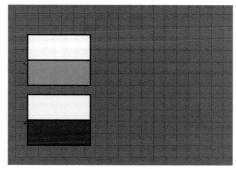

Follow instructions exactly to end up with interlocking seams.

2. Place a second set of strips of **different fabrics**, right sides together, with dark against background. Lock the seams.

3. Sliver trim left end straight.

4. Find the **2½" lines** on the ruler.

5. Cut **two 2½" layered pieces** from each of the paired strips. Cut this many layered pieces:

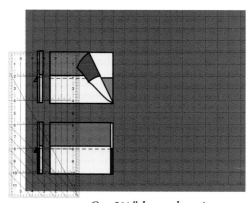

Cut 2½" layered sections.

Quilt Size	Pieces
Wallhanging	32
Crib	48
Lap Robe	96
Twin	120
Dble-Queen	160
King	200

6. Assembly-line sew layered pieces with dark/medium at the top.

7. Place Four-Patch on pressing mat with seam across the bottom. Set the seam. Open and press. Clip threads.

Sew with dark at top. Seams match best when sewn like this. They will also lock when sewing the block together.

8. Measure several Four-Patches. They should measure approximately 4½" square.

Your measurement

_____"

Making Pieced Squares

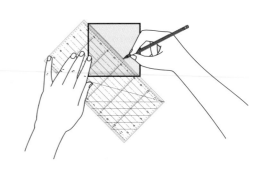

1. Cut remaining 5½" background strips into 5½" squares.

Quilt Size	Squares
Wallhanging	16
Crib	24
Lap Robe	48
Twin	60
Dble-Queen	80
King	100

2. Draw a diagonal line on the wrong side of each one.

3. Place a background square right sides together to a dark/medium square.

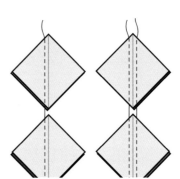

4. Sew a ¼" seam on left side of diagonal line.

5. Place a second pair after the first, and sew a ¼" seam.

6. Assembly-line sew all squares.

7. Turn and sew on second side of diagonal line.

8. Cut on the diagonal line.

9. Lay the triangle on the pressing mat, dark side up. Press to set seam.

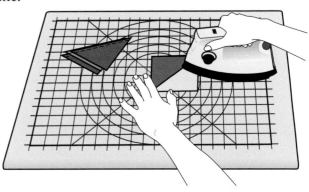

10. Open and press seam to dark side.

11. With a 6" x 6" ruler, square one Pieced Square to the size of your Four-Patch.

    Center the ruler's diagonal line on the seam, and trim two edges.

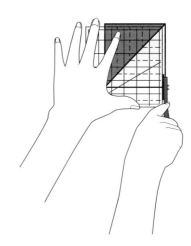

12. Turn the Pieced Square and lay the diagonal line on the seam.

    If your Four-Patch is 4⅜", place the 4⅜" ruler lines on the newly cut edges. Trim the final edges.

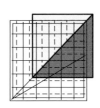

    If your Four-Patch is 4½", place the 4½" ruler lines on the newly cut edges. Trim the final edges.

13. Compare with Four-Patch.

    Be satisfied with size of Pieced Square before trimming all of the pieces.

14. Square up this many Pieced Squares for your size quilt:

Quilt Size	Pieced Squares
Wallhanging	32
Crib	48
Lap Robe	96
Twin	120
Dble-Queen	160
King	200

Sewing Blocks

Sewing Pairs

1. Lay out stacks of Pieced Squares and stacks of Four-Patches. Each piece should be a different color and/or a different fabric.

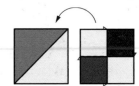

Be sure they are turned correctly

2. Flip a Four-Patch to the Pieced Square, matching the outside edges.

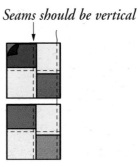

Seams should be vertical

3. Assembly-line sew stacks, pushing seam allowances of Four-Patches as they were pressed.

4. Clip apart in chains of four.

5. Drop on pressing mat with Four-Patch on the top. Set the seam.

6. Lift open and press flat, seam toward Four-Patch. Clip threads.

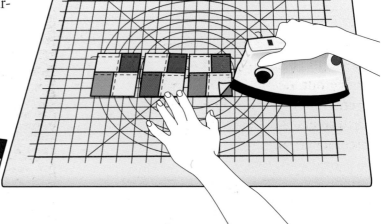

7. Turn patch over. **Press vertical seams toward each other.** Seams will then lock when sewing block together.

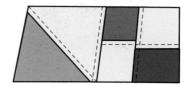

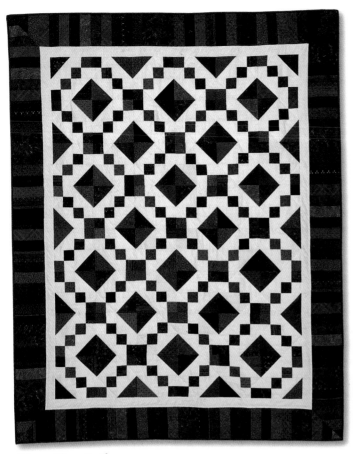

Hour Glass Quilt

Options

If you want a balanced look between values and colors, try the "hour glass" layout.

When sewing quarter blocks, page 34, consistently place a medium pieced square in one corner, and dark Pieced Square in the opposite corner.

When sewing blocks together, place mediums across from each other, and darks across from each other.

If the random placement of pieces appears "too busy" to your eye, try placing four identical Pieced Squares together for a "planned look". The Four-Patches will still have a random, or scrappy look.

Turn to page 57 if you want a "planned look," and follow those instructions.

Planned Quilt by Louise Bosteter

Sewing Quarter Blocks

1. Lay out pairs of Four-Patches /Pieced Squares. Check to see that the combinations are pleasing. Continue stacking all pieces. Be sure they are turned correctly.

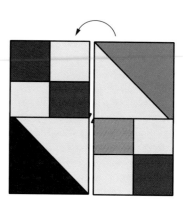

2. Flip the right piece to the left. Leave seam allowances as pressed. At center, fingerpress seams toward Four-Patches.

3. Assembly-line sew the stacks.

4. Clip apart between blocks.

5. Do not press at this step. Fingerpress in next step.

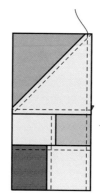

Top seam down.
Bottom seam up.

6. Stack. You need this many Quarter Blocks for your size quilt:

Quilt Size	Quarter Blocks
Wallhanging	16
Crib	24
Lap Robe	48
Twin	60
Dble-Queen	80
King	100

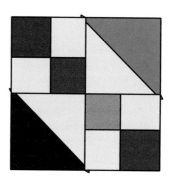

Sewing Four Quarter Blocks into Pattern Blocks

1. Working on a large table, lay out four quarter blocks turned correctly and in a pleasing combination.

2. Lay out a second block next to it. Check to see that there is variety in the fabrics and colors.

3. Continue to lay out the blocks.

   Hour Glass Quilt: In the center, place mediums across from each other, and darks across from each other.

4. Slip one block onto a 16" ruler, and carry to the sewing machine.

5. Flip right pieces to the left. Backstitch. Assembly-line sew, butting the pairs together.

   Optional: Stack and assembly-line sew all vertical seams.

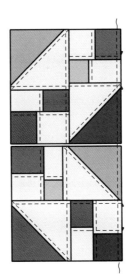

Lock Four-Patch seams.

Fingerpress top seam up and under seam down.

Fingerpress top seam up and under seam down.

Lock Four-Patch seams.

6. Flip the right half to the left.

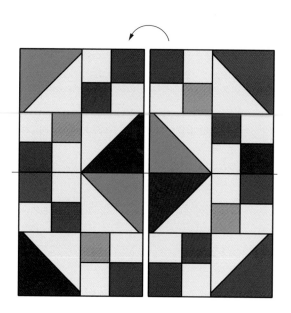

7. Sew horizontal seams, pushing the seams as illustrated.

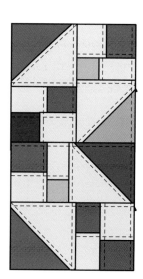

8. From the wrong side, press seams as they were sewn. Press final seam to either side.

Lock Four-Patch seams.

Top seam up, under seam down.

Top seam up, under seam down.

9. Measure the block and record the size.

_____ "

It should measure approximately 16½"

Top seam up, under seam down.

Lock Four-Patch seams.

10. Place the block back in its planned position.

Sewing the Top Together

1. Lay out the pattern blocks in rows. Turn for pleasing combinations.

Quilt Size	Blocks
Wallhanging	2 x 2
Crib	2 x 3
Lap Robe	3 x 4
Twin	3 x 5
Dble-Queen	4 x 5
King	5 x 5

2. Flip the right row to the left.

3. Stack the pairs with the top pair on top.

4. Assembly-line sew the vertical seam. Fingerpress seams as sewn. Do not clip the connecting threads.

5. Open.

6. Sew the horizontal seams, pushing the vertical seam in opposite directions consistently.

7. Press.

Adding the Framing Border

Framing Border strips must
be 2½" wide strips so piano keys fit.

1. Sew the 2½" Frame strips into one
   long piece.

2. Cut two pieces the length of the quilt
   top plus 2".

3. Pin the middle of the strips to
   the middle of the sides. Leave
   about 1" of strips beyond quilt.
   Pin intermittently.

4. With the Frame underneath,
   sew side strips.

5. Press open.

6. Trim strips even with quilt edges.

7. Cut two pieces from the Frame strip
   the width of the quilt plus 2".

8. Center and pin strips, leaving about 1"
   of strips beyond quilt.

9. With Frame underneath, sew top and
   bottom strips.

10. Trim strips even with quilt edges.

Making Piano Keys Border

1   Count out this many dark/medium half strips, 5½" wide by at least 20" long:

Quilt Size	Half Strips
Wallhanging	12
Crib	20
Lap Robe	24
Twin	28
Dble-Queen	32
King	32

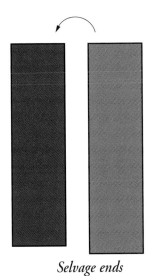

Selvage ends

If your strips are 2½" wide, count out twice as many, and sew together in pairs. Turn to page 40.

2. Make two equal stacks with the raw edge at top and the selvage edge at bottom.

3. Flip the right strip to the left.

4. Press together so that they don't shift during sewing. Pin.

5. Assembly-line sew stacks keeping top edges even.

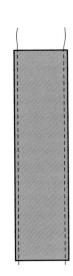

6. Sew the second side of strips in the same direction so they don't distort.

7. Press to set the seams, and clip connecting threads.

8. Place the **2¼" lines** of the 6" x 24" ruler **on the stitching or thread line.** Cut off strip. Stack.

    If you sewed a perfect ¼" seam, the fabric's edge is at 2½".

9. Repeat on the other half. Make second stack.

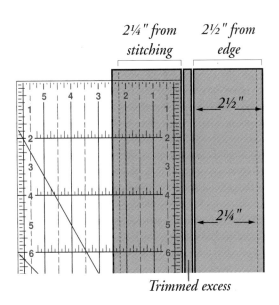

2¼" from stitching   *2½" from edge*

Trimmed excess

10. Place a closed strip on the ironing board with the raw, even end at the left and selvage end at the right. Press open, seam allowances toward the strip on top.

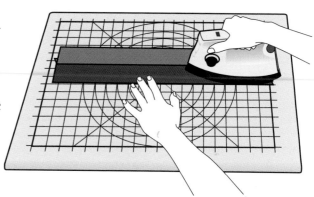

11. Measure. These strips should measure the same width as the Four-Patch.

12. Press open all of the sewn pairs of piano key strips.

13. Stack with raw edges in same direction.

Making the Piano Key Sets

1. Lay out four pairs of strips with raw edges even at the top.

2. Sew the pairs together lengthwise keeping the top edge even.

3. Repeat with remaining strips in groups of four.

4. From the wrong side, press the seams to the left. Make sure there are no folds or tucks at the seam lines.

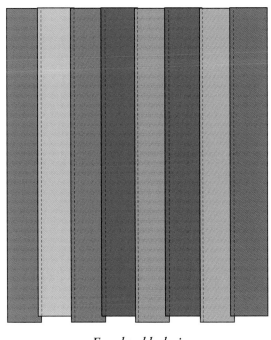

Quilt Size	Sets of 8
Wallhanging	3
Crib	5
Lap Robe	6
Twin	7
Dble-Queen	8
King	8

The width of the eight sewn together should equal the width of your block.

If they are not equal, sliver trim the outside edges to equal the size of the block, or let out seams.

Equal to block size

5. Using the gridded cutting mat, sliver-trim to straighten the even, raw edge.

6. Cut into strips according to your size quilt.

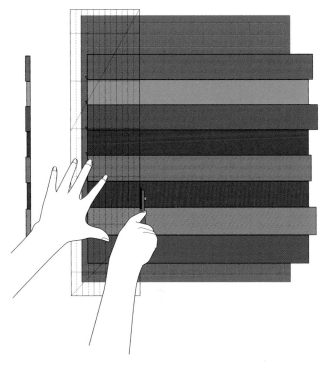

Wallhanging	4½" Strips
Wallhanging	12
Turn to page 42.	

Turn to page 42.

Larger Quilts	6½" Strips
Crib	14
Lap Robe	18
Twin	20
Dble-Queen	22
King	24
Turn to page 43.	

Turn to page 43.

Wallhanging Only
Making the Mitered Corner Blocks

1. Count out three different 4½" wide strips.

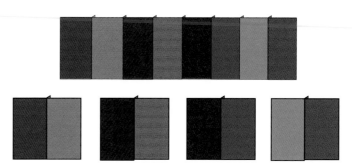

2. Unsew each into four groups of "two keys." Press. Put aside four "two keys" for the four sides of the quilt.

3. Draw a diagonal line on four "two keys".

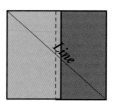

Draw a diagonal line on "two keys".

4. Place a marked "two keys" right sides together to a second "two keys". Place so seams go in opposite directions. Lock seams.

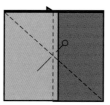

Stitch on diagonal line

5. Pin on the line at seam, and match to the seam underneath.

6. Sew on the line. Put aside.

   Depending on which way the Corner Block is opened, different fabrics dominate. Make that decision and cut away excess when you know which fabric keys along the sides will meet the corners.

Larger Quilts
Making the Mitered Corner Blocks

1. Count out four different 6½" wide strips. Use any sections that have strips shorter than 6½".

2. Unsew each into two groups of "three keys" and one group of "two keys." Press. Put aside the four "two keys" for the four sides of the quilt. The "three keys" are for the mitered corners.

3. Draw a diagonal line on four "three keys".

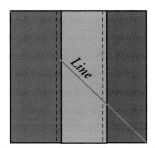

Draw a diagonal line on "three keys".

4. Place a marked "three keys" right sides together to a second "three keys". Place so seams go in opposite directions. Lock seams.

5. Pin on the line at seam, and match to the seam underneath.

6. Sew on the line. Put aside.

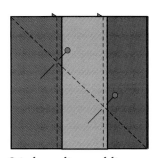

Stitch on diagonal line.

Depending on which way the Corner Block is opened, different fabrics dominate. Make that decision and cut away excess when you know which fabric keys along the sides will meet the corners.

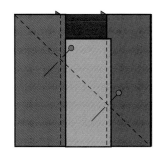

Helpful Hint: Use any pieces with strips shorter than 6½". They will be trimmed away.

Sewing Left and Right Piano Keys to the Quilt

1. Sew together this many strips for each side:

Quilt Size	Strips
Wallhanging	2
Crib	3
Lap Robe	4
Twin	5
Dble-Queen	5
King	5

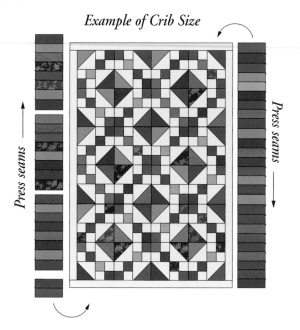

Example of Crib Size

2. Add "two keys" to each strip.

3. Repress the keys so the seams point down when sewing keys to Frame.

4. Flip keys to quilt.

5. Pin, lining up key seams with the block seams.

   If the keys are too long, take a deeper seam on any of the keys.

   If the keys are too short, let out seams on keys.

6. Sew with keys on top.

7. Press seam toward the Frame.

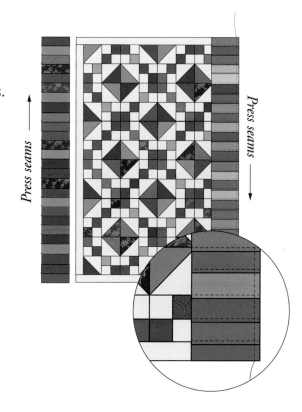

Top and Bottom

1. Sew together this many strips for the top and the bottom:

Quilt Size	Strips
Wallhanging	2
Crib	2
Lap Robe	3
Twin	3
Dble-Queen	4
King	5

2. Add "two keys" to each strip.

3. Lay the top and bottom keys in place.

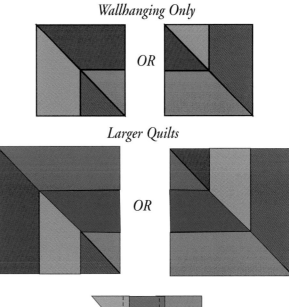

Adding the Corner Blocks

1. Plan Corner Block placement. Depending on which way it is opened, different fabrics dominate.

   Place the squares in the corners. Flip each square to find the best placement.

Wallhanging Only

OR

Larger Quilts

OR

2. Cut away excess fabric ¼" from the stitching after you decide the placement.

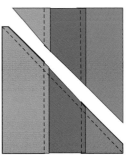

3. Lay trimmed Corner Blocks in place.

   The long pieces on the Corner Blocks are placed next to the piano keys.

4. Sew Corner Blocks to the keys.

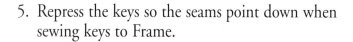

Press seams ⟶

5. Repress the keys so the seams point down when sewing keys to Frame.

6. Flip keys strip to quilt.

7. Pin, lining up key seams with the block seams.

8. Sew with keys on top.

9. Press seam toward the Frame.

Press seams ⟵

10. Stay stitch the outside edges within the ¼" seam allowance to keep key seams from separating.

Finishing

Piecing Queen and King Borders and Binding

1. Stack and square off the ends of each strip, trimming away the selvage edges.

2. Seam the strips of each fabric into long pieces by assembly-line sewing.

   Lay the first strip right side up. Lay the second strip right sides to it. Backstitch, stitch the short ends together, and backstitch again.

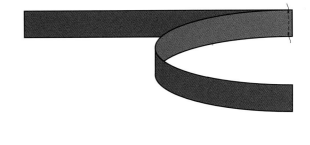

3. Take the strip on the top and fold it so the right side is up.

4. Place the third strip right sides to it, backstitch, stitch, and backstitch again.

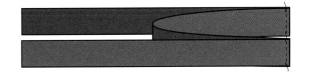

5. Continue assembly-line sewing all the short ends together into long pieces for each fabric.

6. Clip the threads holding the strips together.

7. Press seams to one side.

Sewing Queen and King Borders to the Quilt Top

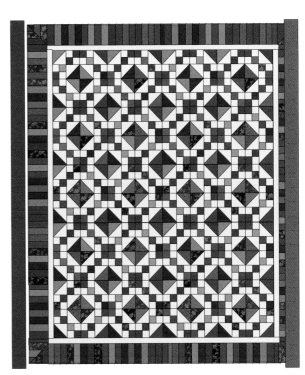

1. Measure down the center to find the length. Cut two side strips that measurement plus 2".

2. Right sides together, match and pin the center of the strips to the center of the sides. Pin at ends, allowing an extra inch of border at each end. Pin intermittently. Sew with the quilt on top. Set and direct the seams, pressing toward the borders.

3. Square the ends even with the top and bottom of the quilt.

4. Measure the width across the center including newly added borders. Cut two strips that measurement plus 2".

5. Right sides together, match and pin the center of the strips to the center of the top and bottom edges of the quilt. Pin at the ends, allowing an extra inch of border at both ends. Pin intermittently. Sew with the quilt on top.

6. Set and direct the seams, pressing toward the borders. Square the ends even with the side borders.

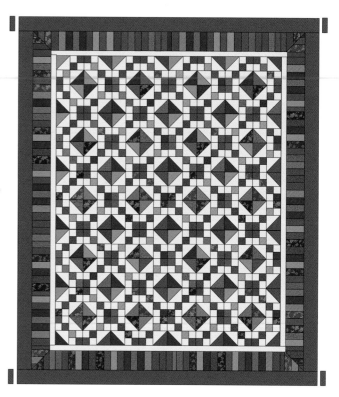

Preparing the Backing

1. Refer to your Yardage Chart for the number of pieces to cut the backing into.

2. Fold the backing crosswise and cut into equal pieces. If you custom fitted your quilt, you may need to adjust these measurements.

3. Tear off the selvages and seam the pieces together.

4. Press the seams to one side.

Piecing the Bonded Batting

1. If the batting needs to be pieced to get the desired size, cut and butt the two straight edges together without overlapping.

2. Hand whipstitch the edges together with a double strand of thread. Do not pull the threads too tightly.

Layering

1. Lay out the backing right side down on a large floor area or table. Tape down on a floor area or clamp onto a table with large binder clips.

2. Place the batting on top and smooth.

3. Lay the quilt top right side up and centered on top of the batting.

4. Completely smooth all layers until they are flat.

5. Tape or clamp securely.

Batting
Clamps
Backing

Plan Your Machine Quilting

Decide how you will machine quilt before you safety pin baste the layers together. There are a number of different ways to machine quilt the Jewel Box quilt. See pages 50-53.

❖ Stitch in the Chain
❖ Stitch around the Four Square
❖ Diagonal Grid Quilting

Place safety pins throughout the quilt away from the planned quilting lines. Begin pinning in the center and work to the outside, spacing pins every 5". Pin the framing border and piano keys.

Grasp the opened pin in your right hand and the pinning tool in your left hand. Push the pin through the three layers, and bring the tip of the pin back out. Catch the tip in the groove of the tool. Push pin closed.

After the pinning is completed, trim the backing and batting to 2" on all sides.

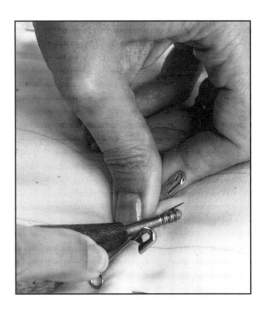

Stitch in the Chain

If you have used a variety of colors in your Four-Patches, you may want to use invisible thread on the top of your sewing machine, and bobbin thread to match your backing. You can draw on the diagonal lines through the Four-Patch, or simply eyeball them as you stitch. This quilting design is easy to do on all sizes of quilts using a walking foot. If you only stitch in the chain, quilting lines will be 11" apart.

Stitch Around the Four Square

If you do this in combination with stitching in the chain, quilting lines will be 2½" apart. You can either "stitch in the ditch" around the Four Square, or outline stitch ¼" away. On small quilts, you can easily stitch around the Four Square with a walking foot. However, larger quilts are difficult to pivot and turn as you stitch. An alternative is to "stitch in the ditch" with your feed dogs disengaged, and use a darning or embroidery foot in place of your walking foot. See page 53. This "free motion" method allows bulky quilts to be stitched side to side as well as forward and backward with little manipulation.

Stitch in the Chain Quilting Diagram

Anchor the center of the quilt first, and then quilt to the outside edges. Follow the numbers for the quilting order.

Place pins in the background on both sides of the dark/medium chain and in the centers of the Four Square.

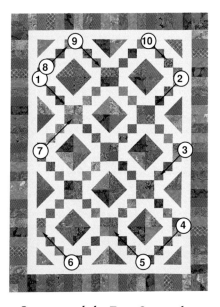

Sew around the Four Square last.

Diagonal Grid Quilting

Quilting lines are 5½" apart over all the quilt. You can draw or eyeball the diagonal lines through the background squares, and "stitch in the ditch" in the Four Square seam. You may choose to use either invisible thread or thread to match your background fabric. This quilting design is easy to do on all sizes of quilts using a walking foot.

Place pins in the dark/medium chain and Four Square.

Diagonal Grid Quilting Diagram

Anchor the center of the quilt first, and then quilt to the outside edges. Follow the numbers for the quilting order.

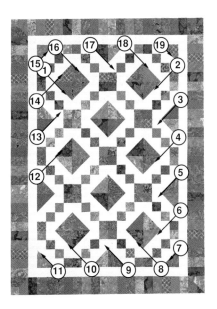

Marking (Optional)

"Crease" lines with a Hera Marker, or mark lines with chalk or silver pencil, and a 6" x 24" ruler.

Stitch in the Chain: Draw the lines through the chain created by the Four-Patches.

Hera Marker

Diagonal Grid Quilting: Line up the ruler with the edges of the Four Square. Draw connecting lines on the background squares.

Machine Set Up for Walking Foot

Place a walking foot attachment on your machine. For Stitch in the Chain, use invisible thread in the top and loosen the top tension. For Diagonal Grid Quilting, use invisible thread or thread to match your background fabric. Place regular thread in the bobbin to match your backing. Lengthen your stitch to 8 - 10 stitches per inch, or a #3 or #4 setting. Use a plexiglass table around free arm machines.

Diagonal Grid and Stitching in the Chain

1. Roll the quilt tightly from the outside edge diagonally in toward the middle. Hold this roll with clips.

2. Slide this roll into the keyhole of the sewing machine.

3. Place the needle in the depth of the framing border seam and pull up the bobbin thread. Lock the stitches by backstitching and clip the threads.

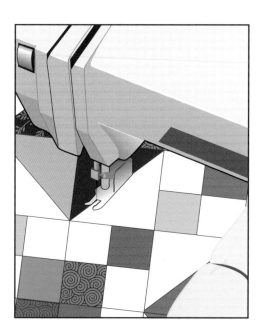

4. Place your hands flat in a triangular shape on both sides of the needle. Stitch forward either on the marked lines, or eyeball the lines of your planned design. Keep the quilt area flat and tight. To keep the weight off the quilting area, hold the rest of the quilt on your lap, or place on your shoulder.

5. Sew the diagonal of the quilt.

6. Unroll, roll, and machine quilt on all diagonal lines following the diagram for your quilt design.

7. Stitch in the seams of the framing border, or ¼" away.

Quilting the Four Square in Small Quilts

1. Use the walking foot. Place the needle in the depth of the seam, or ¼" away from the seam. Backstitch and trim threads.

2. At each corner, pivot with the needle in the fabric. Turn to the next side.

3. Backstitch and trim threads.

Quilting the Four Square in Large Quilts

Place a darning foot, embroidery foot, or spring needle on your machine, and drop the feed dogs or cover with a plate. Use a fine needle and a little hole throat plate. Use invisible thread or thread to match the background on top, and thread to match the backing in the bobbin. Loosen the top tension if using invisible thread.

1. Drop the needle in the depth of the seam. Bring up the bobbin thread.

2. Lower the needle and drop the foot. Lock stitches by moving back and forth in the seam, and clip threads.

3. Stretch the fabric with your fingertips. Run the machine at a constant speed while moving the fabric in a steady motion. Watch the outline of the Four Square ahead of the needle. Keep the top of the quilt in the same position by moving the fabric underneath the needle forward, side to side, and backward.

4. Lock off the stitches, pull up the bobbin thread, and clip.

Adding the Binding

See Piecing Strips, page 47.

1. Place a walking foot attachment on your sewing machine. Use regular thread on top and in the bobbin to match the binding. Set your machine for 10 stitches per inch, or #3 setting.

2. Press the binding strip in half lengthwise with right sides out.

3. Line up the raw edges of the folded binding with the raw edge of the quilt top at the middle of one side.

4. Begin sewing 4" from the end of the binding.

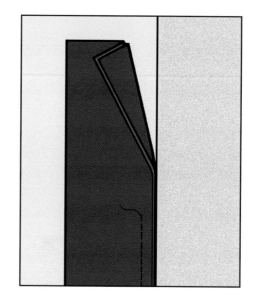

5. At the corner, stop the stitching ¼" from the edge with the needle in the fabric. Raise the presser foot and turn the quilt to the next side. Put the foot back down.

6. Sew backwards ¼" to the edge of the binding, raise the foot, and pull the quilt forward slightly.

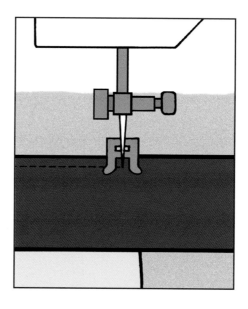

7. Fold the binding strip straight up on the diagonal. Fingerpress in the diagonal fold.

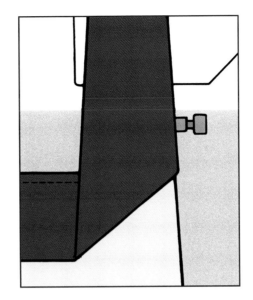

8. Fold the binding strip straight down with the diagonal fold underneath. Line up the top of the fold with the raw edge of the binding underneath.

9. Begin sewing from the corner.

10. Continue sewing and mitering the corners around the outside of the quilt.

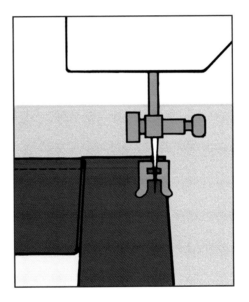

11. Stop sewing 4" from where the ends will overlap.

12. Line up the two ends of binding. Trim the excess with a ½" overlap.

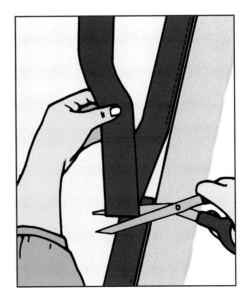

13. Open out the folded ends and pin right sides together. Sew a ¼" seam.

14. Continue to sew the binding in place.

15. Trim the batting and backing up to the raw edges of the binding.

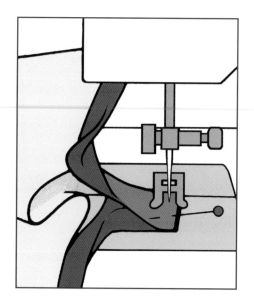

16. Fold the binding to the back side of the quilt. Pin in place so that the folded edge on the binding covers the stitching line. Tuck in the excess fabric at each miter on the diagonal.

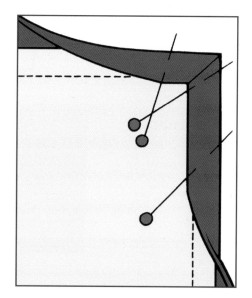

17. From the right side, "stitch in the ditch" using invisible thread on the right side, and a bobbin thread to match the binding on the back side. Catch the folded edge of the binding on the back side with the stitching.

Optional: Hand slip stitch.

18. Sew an identification label on the back listing your name, date, and other pertinent information.

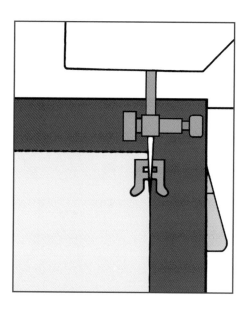

Planned Jewel Box (optional)

If the random placement of pieces appears "too busy" to your eye, try placing four identical Pieced Squares together for a "planned look". The Four-Patches will still have a random, or scrappy look.

1. Stack pairs with four identical pieced squares.

2. Create pattern on floor or table by turning all four pieced squares together in one block.

3. Build new blocks off the corners.

4. Lay out the whole quilt.

5. Slip one block onto 16" Square Up. Sew quarters together. See page 34.

6. Sew block together, following instructions on pages 35 and 36.

7. Put block back into pattern layout.

Four Block Miniature Quilt

Instructions are given for using 2", 3", or 4" charm squares or squares cut from scraps. However, utilizing the mathematical equations, any size charm squares can be used. If edges of charm squares are pinked, it's not necessary to trim them before sewing. Add regular borders in place of piano key borders.

Sq. Size	Quilt Size
2" squares	15"
3" squares	22"
4" squares	35"

Large charm squares can be cut into smaller squares for smaller quilts. For instance, cut 6" squares into four 3" squares, or nine 2" squares, and 4" squares into four 2" squares.

Quilter's Candy, a set of sixteen different 2" fabric samples, is packaged by Benartex. For each quilt, you need thirty-two different medium or dark squares, plus light background strips cut selvage to selvage the same measurement as the squares. Border and binding strips are also cut selvage to selvage.

	2" Squares	3" Squares	4" Squares
Medium and Dark	(32) 2" squares	(32) 3" squares	(32) 4" squares
Background Strips	(2) 2" wide strips	(3) 3" wide strips	(4) 4" wide strips
First Border	(1) 1" wide strip	(2) 1½" wide strips	(2) 2" wide strips
Second Border	(2) 2" wide strips	(3) 3½" wide strips	(4) 4½" wide strip
Backing and Batting	18" squares	25" squares	38" squares
Binding	(2) 2¼" wide strips	(3) 2¼" wide strips	(4) 2¾" strips

Getting Started

1. Cut light background strips selvage to selvage the same size as the medium and dark squares.

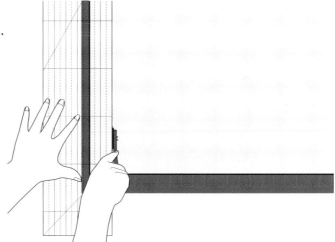

2. Divide the medium and dark squares into two equal stacks. Make sure colors are divided evenly between the two stacks.

3. Thread your machine with a color slighter darker than the background color.

4. Set your machine with a **scant ¼" seam allowance** by moving the needle position slightly to the right.

sixteen squares for the Four-Patch   *sixteen squares for the Pieced Squares*

Making Four-Patches

Sewing Squares to Background Strips

1. Place light background strip right side up on sewing machine.

2. Place square right sides together to strip. Sew a **scant ¼" seam**, and 15 stitches per inch, or a #2 setting.

3. Place second square next to first square, and sew scant ¼" seam. Continue to sew sixteen squares in same manner. Start new strips as necessary until all squares are sewn.

4. Turn strip, and sew scant ¼" seam on second side.

5. Press to set seams.

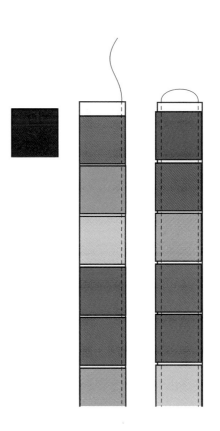

Cutting Pieces

1. Place the lines on the 6" x 12" ruler on the stitching lines according to your size square. Cut.

    2" squares - ¾" lines
    3" squares - 1¼" lines
    4" squares - 1¾" lines

    Calculation is half of original square size, minus ¼".

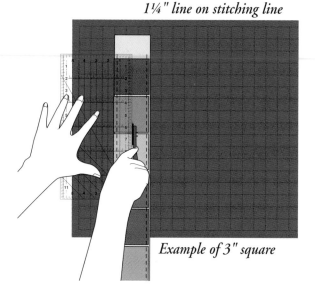

1¼" line on stitching line

Example of 3" square

2. Repeat on the other half, placing the ruler lines on the stitching lines.

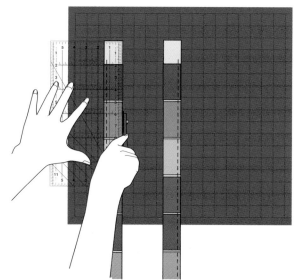

3. Lay on the ironing board with medium and dark rectangles on top. Press open, seam allowance to the dark side.

4. With a 6" square ruler, cut apart between the rectangles. The widths of the pieces should now be ½" smaller than the original size square.

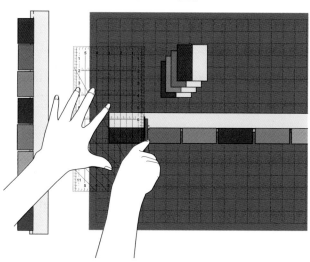

5. Place a set of strips on the cutting mat, with light sides up.

6. Place a second set of strips with different fabrics right sides together with the dark against the background. Lock the seams.

7. With 6" x 6" ruler, layer cut pairs according to your original size square.

> **2" squares - 1" pieces**
> **3" squares - 1½" pieces**
> **4" squares - 2" pieces**

Calculation is half of the original size square.

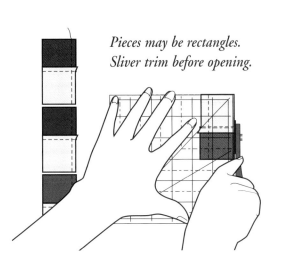

8. Assembly-line sew.

9. Place the lines on the 6" x 6" ruler on the stitching lines according to your original size square. Sliver trim if necessary.

> **2" squares - ¾" lines**
> **3" squares - 1¼" lines**
> **4" squares - 1¾" lines**

Calculation is half of original square size, minus ¼".

Pieces may be rectangles. Sliver trim before opening.

10. Press open.

11. Measure and record. Four-patch should be square.

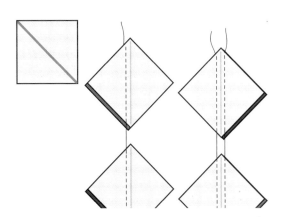

"
_____

Making Pieced Squares

1. Cut remaining background strips into 16 squares. With a pencil, draw diagonal lines on wrong side of each one.

2. Place marked squares right sides together to dark/medium squares. Pin.

3. Sew **scant** ¼" on left side of diagonal line.

4. Sew on second side of diagonal lines.

5. Press to set seams.

6. Cut apart on diagonal lines.

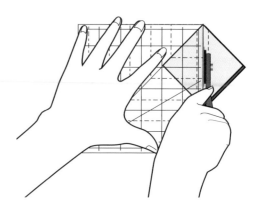

7. Open and press seams to dark side.

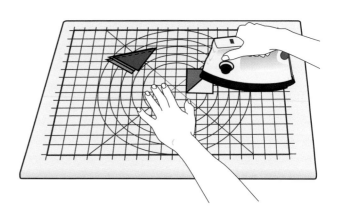

8. Square pieces to same size as Four-Patch.

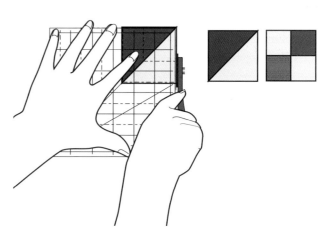

Finishing the Miniature Quilt

1. Sew pieces into four blocks. See pages 32-38.

2. Add borders. See pages 47-48.

3. Machine quilt and bind. See pages 50-56.

Acknowledgements

Many thanks to Selim Benardete, of Benartex Fabrics, and to his wonderful staff. I would like to congratulate designers Patricia Campbell and Michelle Jack for their lovely Impressions line of fabric, which has been perfect for the Jewel Box. Quilt in a Day's association with Benartex continues to be a mutually inspiring development for both companies.

A special thanks to my "test class" students! Your questions and insights were a great help, and your beautiful quilts were an inspiration. I am especially grateful to Judy Pedersen, Betty Carruthers, Loretta Smith, Louise Bosteter, Patricia Knoechel, and Sue Bouchard for allowing their quilts to be pictured in the Jewel Box book and video.

Index

● Order Information

Quilt in a Day books offer a wide range of techniques and are directed toward a variety of skill levels. If you do not have a quilt shop in your area, you may write or call for a complete catalog and current price list of all books and patterns published by Quilt in a Day®, Inc.

Easy

These books are easy enough for beginners of any age.

Quilt in a Day Log Cabin
Irish Chain in a Day
Bits & Pieces Quilt
Trip Around the World Quilt
Heart's Delight Wallhanging
Scrap Quilt, Strips and Spider Webs
Rail Fence Quilt
Dresden Placemats
Flying Geese Quilt
Star for all Seasons Placemats
Winning Hand Quilt
Courthouse Steps Quilt
From Blocks to Quilt

Applique

While these offer a variety of techniques, easy applique is featured in each.

Applique in a Day
Dresden Plate Quilt
Sunbonnet Sue Visits Quilt in a Day
Recycled Treasures
Country Cottages and More
Creating with Color
Spools & Tools Wallhanging
Dutch Windmills Quilt

Intermediate to Advanced

With a little Quilt in a Day experience, these books offer a rewarding project.

Trio of Treasured Quilts
Lover's Knot Quilt
Amish Quilt
May Basket Quilt
Morning Star Quilt
Friendship Quilt
Kaleidoscope Quilt
Machine Quilting Primer

Tulip Quilt
Star Log Cabin Quilt
Burgoyne Surrounded Quilt
Bird's Eye Quilt
Snowball Quilt
Tulip Table Runner

Holiday

When a favorite holiday is approaching, Quilt in a Day is there to help you plan.

Country Christmas
Bunnies & Blossoms
Patchwork Santa
Last Minute Gifts
Angel of Antiquity
Log Cabin Wreath Wallhanging
Log Cabin Christmas Tree Wallhanging
Country Flag
Lover's Knot Placemats

Sampler

Always and forever popular are books with a variety of patterns.

The Sampler
Block Party Series 1, Quilter's Year
Block Party Series 2, Baskets & Flowers
Block Party Series 3, Quilters Almanac
Block Party Series 4, Christmas Traditions
Block Party Series 5, Pioneer Sampler

Angle Piecing

Quilt in a Day "template free" methods make angle cutting less of a challenge.

Diamond Log Cabin Tablecloth or Treeskirt
Pineapple Quilt
Blazing Star Tablecloth
Schoolhouse Quilt
Radiant Star Quilt

Quilt in a Day®, Inc. • 1955 Diamond Street, • San Marcos, CA 92069
Toll Free: 1 800 777-4852 • Fax: (619) 591-4424
Internet: http://www.quilt-in-a-day.com/qiad/ • 8 am to 5 pm Pacific Time